THE PLANETARY SOCIETY

T0112995

EARTH

OUR HOME PLANET

Bruce Betts, PhD

Lerner Publications ◆ Minneapolis

THE PLANETS AND MOONS IN OUR SOLAR SYSTEM ARE OUT OF THIS WORLD. Some are hotter than an oven, and some are much colder than a freezer. Some are small and rocky, while others are huge and mostly made of gas. As you explore these worlds, you'll discover giant canyons, active volcanoes, strange kinds of ice, storms bigger than Earth, and much more.

The Planetary Society® empowers people around the world to advance space science and exploration. On behalf of The Planetary Society®, including our tens of thousands of members, here's wishing you the joy of discovery.

Onward,

Bill Nye
CEO, The Planetary Society®

TABLE OF CONTENTS

CHAPTER 1

OUR HOME PLANET

Earth is our home planet. It is where you are right now. It has wide oceans, big stretches of land, and clouds in the sky. It has freezing ice and burning lava. It is the third planet from the Sun. And it is the only place we know of that has life.

Astronauts in space can see huge clouds move across Earth.

Distances in space are measured using astronomical units (AU). One AU is equal to the average distance between Earth and the Sun, which is about 93 million miles (150 million km).

EARTH FAST FACTS

Size	7,900 miles (12,714 km) wide
Distance from the Sun	about 93 million miles (150 million km)
Length of day	twenty-four hours
Length of year	365.25 days
Number of moons	one

Earth Is Just Right

Earth orbits the Sun. That means it goes around the Sun in a circle. Some planets are very hot because they are close

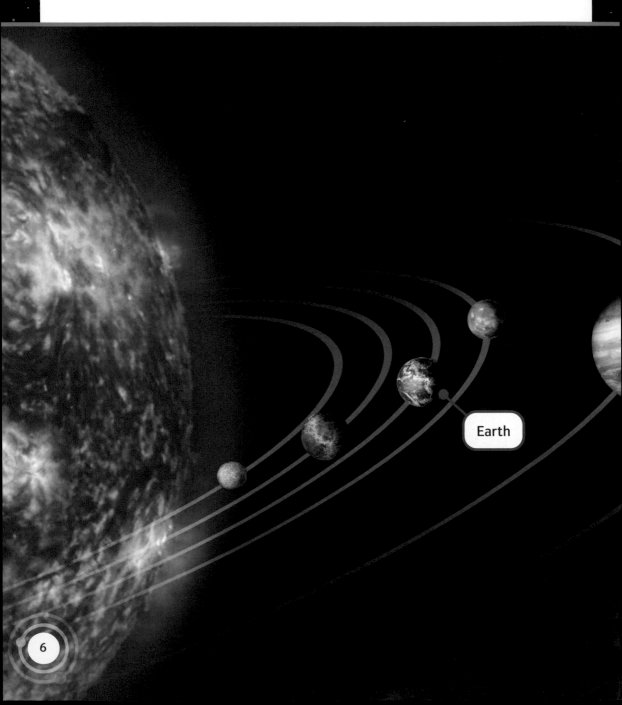

Earth

to the Sun. Others are very cold because they are far away from it. Earth is just the right temperature for life to survive on the planet.

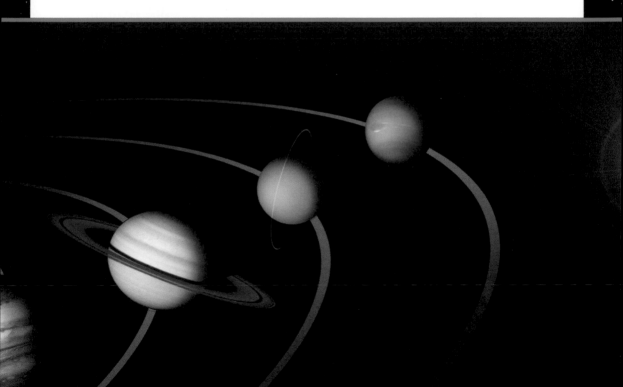

A day on Earth is twenty-four hours long. A day is the time a planet takes to fully spin around from one noon to the next noon. When you are on the side of Earth lit up by the Sun, it is daytime. When you are on the other side, it is nighttime.

A year is the time it takes a planet to go all the way around the Sun. One Earth year is about 365 days long.

The side of Earth that is facing the Sun is in daytime.

ROCKY AND GIANT PLANETS

Mercury, Venus, Earth, and Mars are the four planets closest to the Sun. They are called the inner planets or the rocky planets. They all have rocky surfaces. Earth is the biggest of the rocky planets.

The four planets farthest from the Sun are Jupiter, Saturn, Uranus, and Neptune. They are called the outer planets or the giant planets. They are much larger than the rocky planets. They are also made of gas. They have no ground to stand on.

Left to right: Mercury, Venus, Earth, and Mars are the four rocky planets. Earth is the largest.

Many planets have moons. Moons are small planetlike objects that orbit a planet. The word *moon* came from the name we gave our moon in English, the Moon.

The Moon is big, bright, and circular in the night sky. It goes everywhere Earth goes. Earth and the Moon orbit the Sun together. The Moon is much smaller than Earth. If Earth were the size of a basketball, the Moon would be about the size of a tennis ball.

The Moon is one-quarter as wide as Earth.

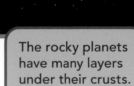

The rocky planets have many layers under their crusts.

Earth has a metal center called the core. The planets were very hot when they formed. They were mostly liquid rock, like lava. Metals such as iron sank to the middle of the planets and formed the cores.

CHAPTER 2

LIVING EARTH

Earth is special because it has everything needed to support all kinds of life. Earth is home to plants, bacteria, and fungi. It is also home to animals, including we humans!

Earth has some important things that are different from all the other planets in the solar system. These include tectonic plates, oxygen, and liquid water.

Earth rising over the Moon's horizon

Tectonic Plates

Earth's surface is made up of tectonic plates. These plates are huge pieces of Earth that move slowly. They fit together like pieces of a puzzle. Sometimes earthquakes happen when those pieces scrape against one another.

In some places, older rocks and metals get pushed down under the surface by plates. In other places, new material gets pushed up to create mountains. When liquid rock rises to the surface, it can burst out to create a volcano.

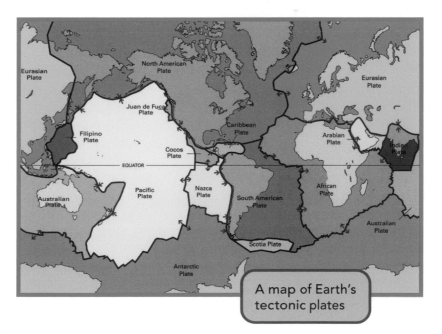

A map of Earth's tectonic plates

OXYGEN

Humans and other animals need to breathe in a gas called oxygen to live. Earth is the only planet with lots of oxygen in its atmosphere.

This is because of plants. Plants take in a gas called carbon dioxide to grow. They turn some of this carbon dioxide into oxygen. We breathe in that oxygen and breathe out carbon dioxide. Then it all happens again!

Astronauts in orbit around Earth can see Earth's blue atmosphere from the side, and sometimes they can also see the Moon.

Hot Air

Our atmosphere keeps us safe from some dangers in space, such as meteoroids. Meteoroids are small rocks in space. They move so fast that they usually burn up when they hit the gas in our atmosphere. Most never hit the ground.

From space, we can see all of Earth's oceans and continents.

The sky looks blue because Earth's atmosphere is mostly made of the gases nitrogen and oxygen. Most colors of light don't bounce off these gases as much, but blue light does. That blue light is what we see in the sky.

Every living thing on Earth needs water, including you!

LIFE NEEDS WATER

Some planets and moons have water on their surface. But that water is in the form of gas or frozen ice. Only Earth has liquid water on its surface all the time. Liquid water is one of the few things that all life on Earth needs.

From space, Earth looks mostly blue and white. It is blue because of the oceans and white because of the clouds. Most of Earth's surface is covered with oceans. More than two-thirds of the surface is covered with liquid water.

Life takes many forms on Earth.

CHAPTER 3

EXPLORING EARTH

For most of our history, humans have studied Earth by exploring its land and seas. But now scientists can learn a lot by studying our planet using spacecraft that orbit Earth. These are called satellites.

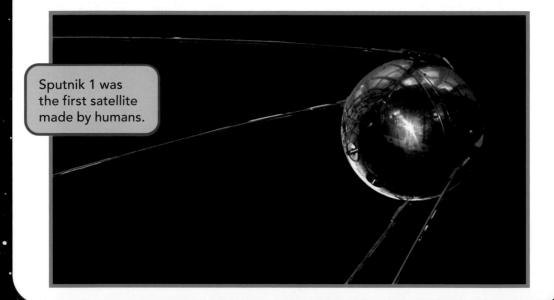

Sputnik 1 was the first satellite made by humans.

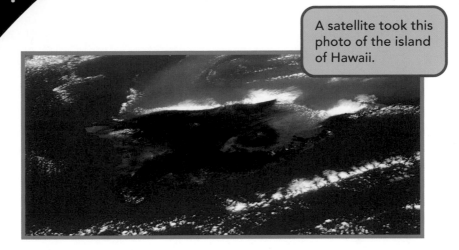

Humans launched the first spacecraft in 1957. We have launched thousands of spacecraft since then. Most of these spacecraft have been satellites.

A few spacecraft have been sent deeper into space to study other planets and moons in the solar system. The spacecraft Voyager 1 was launched into space in 1977. Now it is over 15 billion miles (24 billion km) away from Earth.

Satellites do many things. Some satellites give us different views of mountains, valleys, and lakes. Others have powerful telescopes that look into space. These telescopes have helped scientists find new planets around other stars far away from Earth.

Some satellites help us predict the weather. They can see when a hurricane is forming and where it is moving. Hurricanes are giant storms that can be dangerous to people. Satellites can help people know when a hurricane is coming.

A satellite took this photo of a hurricane on Earth.

Satellites can see volcanoes erupt high into the atmosphere.

Scientists use satellites to learn about the atmosphere, the oceans, and the land on Earth as well as the space around the planet. They also study climate. Climate is how weather patterns change over many years.

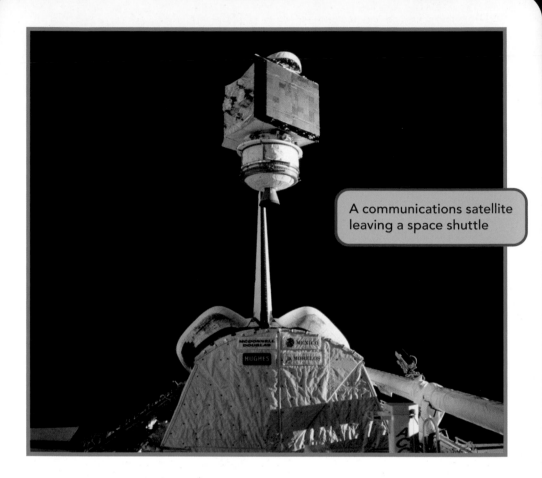

A communications satellite leaving a space shuttle

You may have used satellites without even knowing it. Some people get their TV from satellites using satellite dishes on their roof. These dishes get signals that are sent down from satellites.

When you use a map on a phone, you may be using a satellite. Many maps on phones get information from satellites to show you where you are on the planet.

Pictures from space give us a different view of our home world. They can show large areas of Earth or Earth as a whole. They can show us human activity from space, such as city lights at night.

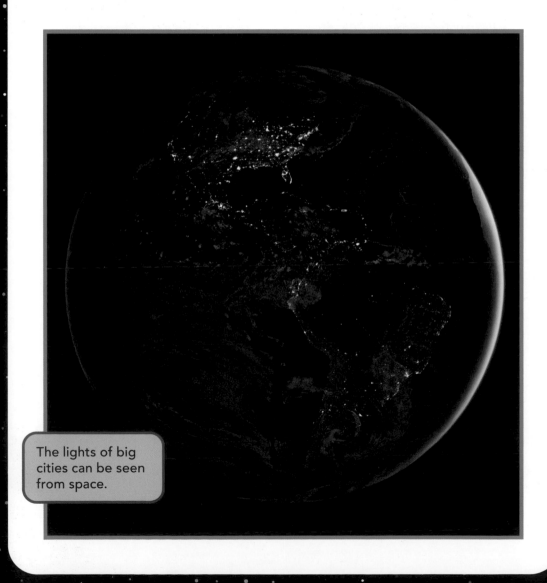

The lights of big cities can be seen from space.

Some humans use spacecraft to go to space and do experiments there. These people are often called astronauts. Astronauts need special spacecraft that provide them with everything they need to survive. That includes oxygen, food, and water.

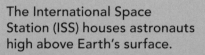

The International Space Station (ISS) houses astronauts high above Earth's surface.

Astronauts launch on rockets in spacecraft made for short trips. They often take those spacecraft to a larger space station that stays in orbit around Earth. One big station in orbit is the International Space Station (ISS). The ISS has held people since 2000. Each astronaut usually spends only a few months on the ISS. They do science experiments and keep the ISS working in orbit around Earth.

Many of the Moon's biggest craters can be seen from Earth.

Our Moon

The Moon reflects light from the Sun. It shines brightly most nights. Sometimes it can even be seen during the day. The Moon is close enough that it looks like a circle and not just a dot in the sky. But it is still far away. About thirty Earths could fit between Earth and the Moon.

The Moon is the only world humans have visited beyond Earth. So far, only twelve astronauts have walked on the Moon since humans first landed there in 1969. Astronauts have brought back rocks and dust from the Moon to study what they are made of. But no one has walked on the Moon since 1972.

Astronaut Buzz Aldrin on the Moon

To the Moon!

More than one hundred spacecraft have been launched toward the Moon. Some orbit the Moon and study it from space. Some have landed. Others have even carried astronauts.

An astronaut visiting a robotic spacecraft that landed on the Moon two years earlier

Astronauts have collected and brought back rock and dirt samples from the Moon for study back on Earth.

THE FUTURE

The future will be an exciting time for Earth and Moon exploration. Many new, advanced spacecraft will study Earth and the Moon. Humans may land on the Moon again in the future.

There is still a lot we don't know about Earth. Scientists are still learning about ocean currents, weather, and climate. And we are still learning more about how Earth's plates have shifted and changed over time.

A photo from a test of the Orion spacecraft that NASA plans to use to take humans from Earth to the Moon

An Orion spacecraft launched on November 16, 2022, on the new Space Launch System rocket.

Earth is a special planet and the only one we know of where humans can survive. By studying Earth and our Moon, we can learn how they formed and changed over time. And we learn about our home and our place in it.

GLOSSARY

astronomical unit (AU): the average distance between Earth and the Sun, about 93 million miles (150 million km)

atmosphere: the gases surrounding a planet, moon, or other body

core: the center of a planet or moon

day: the time it takes a planet to spin around and go from noon to noon. One Earth day is about twenty-four hours long.

moon: an object that orbits a planetary body. Moons are often called natural satellites.

planet: a big, round, ball-shaped object that goes around the Sun. Our solar system has eight planets. A planet is the largest object in or near its orbit.

plate: pieces of Earth's surface that move very slowly over time

spacecraft: a vehicle or object made for travel in outer space

tectonic: relating to the structure of the crust of a planet

LEARN MORE

Britannica Kids: Earth
https://kids.britannica.com/students/article/Earth/274103

Earley, Christina. *Earth Systems*. Coral Springs, FL: Seahorse, 2023.

Golusky, Jackie. *Explore Earth*. Minneapolis: Lerner Publications, 2021.

NASA Space Place: All about Earth
https://spaceplace.nasa.gov/all-about-Earth/en/

The Planetary Society: Earth, Our Home Planet
https://www.planetary.org/worlds/earth

Reynolds, Donna. *Can Humans Live on Other Planets?* Buffalo: Enslow, 2024.

INDEX

PHOTO ACKNOWLEDGMENTS

Image credits: F. Scott Schafer/The Planetary Society, p. 2; NASA/Reid Wiseman, p. 4; NASA/JPL, pp. 6–7, 8, 11; NASA, JHUAPL/CIW, ESA/MPS/UPD/LAM/IAA/RSSD/INTA/UPM/DASP/IDA, p. 9; NASA/JPL Caltech, p. 10; NASA, pp. 12, 14, 15, 19, 20, 21, 23, 24, 26, 27, 28; USGS, p. 13; Bruce Betts, pp. 16, 17; SSDC, NASA, p. 18; NASA/JSC, p. 22; NASA/GSFC/ASU, p. 25; NASA/Bill Ingalls, p.29. Design elements: Sergey Balakhnichev/Getty Images; Baac3nes/Getty Images; Elena Kryulena/Shutterstock; Anna Frajtova/Shutterstock.
Cover: NASA/Reto Stöckli, Render by Robert Simmon.

FOR MY SONS, KEVIN AND DANIEL, AND FOR ALL THE MEMBERS OF THE PLANETARY SOCIETY®

Lerner Publications Company
An imprint of Lerner Publishing Group, Inc.
241 First Avenue North
Minneapolis, MN 55401 USA

For reading levels and more information, look up this title at www.lernerbooks.com.

Main body text set in Aptifer Sans LT Pro. Typeface provided by Linotype AG.

Editor: Cole Nelson **Designer:** Mary Ross

Library of Congress Cataloging-in-Publication Data

Names: Betts, Bruce (PhD), author.
Title: Earth : our home planet / Bruce Betts, PhD.
Description: Minneapolis, MN : Lerner Publications, [2025] | Series: Exploring our solar system with the Planetary Society | Includes bibliographical references and index. | Audience: Ages 7–10 | Audience: Grades 2–3 | Summary: "Earth is our home and the only planet that we know has life. Learn more about our home planet through fun diagrams and colorful photos"— Provided by publisher.
Identifiers: LCCN 2023039508 (print) | LCCN 2023039509 (ebook) | ISBN 9798765626849 (library binding) | ISBN 9798765628614 (paperback) | ISBN 9798765633168 (epub)
Subjects: LCSH: Earth (Planet)—Juvenile literature.
Classification: LCC QB631.4 .B48 2025 (print) | LCC QB631.4 (ebook) | DDC 525—dc23/eng/20231018

LC record available at https://lccn.loc.gov/2023039508
LC ebook record available at https://lccn.loc.gov/2023039509

Manufactured in the United States of America
1-1010100-52015-2/5/2024